101 TIPS FOR HELPING WITH YOUR CHILD'S LEARNING

PROVEN STRATEGIES FOR ACCELERATED LEARNING AND RAISING SMART CHILDREN USING POSITIVE PARENTING SKILLS

BUKKY EKINE-OGUNLANA

TCECPUBLISHING.COM

CONTENTS

Introduction   9

1. Developing Reading Skills   13
2. How To Improve The Spelling Abilities Of Your Child   30
3. Simple Strategies For Teaching Your Child Mathematics At Home   40
4. Teaching your kids English at home   49
5. Homework & Study Skills   58
6. How to Develop an Inquisitive Mind   74
7. Creative Outlets for Kids   81

Conclusion   93
Other Books You'll Love!   95
References   105

© **Copyright Bukky Ekine-Ogunlana 2020 – All rights reserved.**

The content contained within this book may not be reproduced, duplicated or transmitted without direct written permission from the author or the publisher.

Under no circumstance will any blame or legal responsibility be held against the publisher, or author, for any damages, reparation, or monetary loss due to the information contained within this book. Either directly or indirectly. You are responsible for your own choices, actions and results.

Legal Notice:

This book is copyright protected. This book is only for personal use. You cannot amend, distribute, sell, use, quote or paraphrase any part, or the content within this book, without the consent of the author or publisher.

Disclaimer Notice:

Please note the information contained within this document is for educational and entertainment purpose only. All effort has been executed to present accurate, up to date, and reliable, complete information. No warranties of any kind are declared or implied. Readers acknowledge that the author is not engaging in the rendering of legal, financial, medical or professional advice. The content within this book has been derived from various sources. Please consult a licensed professional before attempting any techniques outlined in this book

By reading this document , the reader agrees that under no circumstances is the author responsible for any losses, direct or indirect, which are incurred as a result of the use of the information contained within this document, Including, but not limited to, —errors, omissions, or inaccuracies.

Published by

TCEC Publishing

TCEC House

14-18 Ada Street, London Fields,

E8 4QU, England, Great Britain.

This book is dedicated to our three amazing children (Peace, Joshua and Caleb) and all the beautiful children all over the world who over the years have passed through the T.C.E.C 6-16 years program. Thanks for the opportunity to serve you and invest in your colourful and bright future.

INTRODUCTION

Studies have shown that children are more active and successful in school when parents are interested in their learning and homework [1]. Many resources in books and on the internet will show you that throughout your child's education, a robust family framework that is able to support them is significantly beneficial in how they process new information and further develop their knowledge of critical areas. Of course, helping your children with learning or their homework doesn't require you to spend several hours behind a desk. As a parent, you can develop your child's learning by improving reading and spelling abilities in your child, teaching your child mathematics or English language at home, demonstrating organisation and study skills, or explaining a difficult problem. Improving your child's behaviour at school, giving them the chance to achieve higher grades are some of the benefits you start to gain when you involve yourself with your child's learning [2]. What if getting involved in your child's learning could help to reduce his/her behavioural problems at school, improve his/her grades or help him/her enjoy school the more? Getting involved in your child's learning doesn't demand that you have an educational background or a big fat account. Your involvement in your child's learning will further make him successful at home. Homework time gives you an insight into your child's life at school, giving you the opportunity to see what their day has been about [3].

In addition to improving your child's grade at school, getting involved in your child's learning helps to improve your child's behaviour and social skills at school. Studies have shown that children who are guided by their parents are less likely to be suspended, less likely to skip school, less likely to disrupt the class and less likely to fail a subject.

Children that are supported both at home and school have more self-confidence, they develop positive attitudes about school, and they place much priority on academic achievement. Children do not only benefit when parents are involved in their learning. No, parents also benefits! When parents are involved in their kid's education, they are more confident in their parenting skills, and there's a high possibility for them to continue their education.

This book "101 tips for helping with your child's learning" is written for parents to get involved in their child's education and learning. This book is as a result of my experience as a teacher at the tuition centre; we have a tuition centre where we help children with Mathematics, English, reading and spelling tuition. This book will show the secrets and tactics of teaching to help parents get involved in their children's education. This paperback is divided into five chapters, and each section addresses the tactics and secrets that are required for parents to get involved in their child's learning. Each chapter sums up 101 ways to help develop your child's learning.

Please get in touch and provide us with your honest, unfiltered feedback/review on how useful this book was to you. It will be much appreciated and helpful to hear as many opinions and responses to this book as possible.

1

DEVELOPING READING SKILLS
DEVELOPING READING SKILLS IN CHILDREN

As a teacher, teaching students how to read is one of my passions. In my experience, I found that most children do not start reading until around 4-6 years old. However, the strategies listed in this chapter are helpful for children of all ages. Do not practice these strategies at a go and do not pressurize your child to practice all the strategies immediately. At the tuition centre, we have met with parents who come to ask how they can help their children learn to read at home. This is not a surprise because reading is an essential skill that every child is expected to learn. Reading plays a critical role in the success of a child at school. Teaching children how to read is a process, and the information detailed in this chapter is for you to carry out or practice when your child is ready. I should also mention that although the strategies listed below are labelled as steps, they are not in consecutive order or in the order of importance.

Here are some practical ways by which parents can help their young child or teen learn how to read.

Teaching children how to read

Parents are often told that teaching children how to read at the early years is unwholesome, but this is not entirely true. In fact, the effect of doing so is different in every case, for some it can bring on unnecessary anxiety, but for others it is an opportunity to excel and thrive. Introducing children to engage with and develop literacy skills in their early years isn't harmful, most of the time. I started reading to my children the day I gave birth to them. Studies have shown that the inner ear of a foetus during pregnancy fully develops at 20 weeks. This indicates that your baby is ready to listen and learn from the first day of delivery. As babies grow, they use their hearing to process information about the world around them [4]. Though, the "implications of early teaching" has been studied and discussed for several years; there hasn't been a piece of single evidence to convince readers that reading to children at the early years is harmful. On the flip side, there are several hundreds of studies that show the benefits of reading to children in their early years. When you are reading to your child, you are teaching the child to listen. The child might be looking at your face or not make any move or he might not respond but the child is listening ,when children learn to listen properly, they will learn to decode information accurately.

Why children fail in comprehension is because they have not been well thought on how to listen and interpret what they have read. This must be taught deliberately at home.

Listening is learnt at home and school only takes advantage of it. Teachers assume that children have been taught how to listen from home.

1. Teaching literacy is similar to teaching other essential skills

As a parent, you do not need to get a doctorate to raise healthy, happy and smart children. Parents have been in the business of teaching their children how to read since the dawn of time, or at least when the first book was written. Teaching literacy to children is in no way groundbreaking and we're not about to re-invent the wheel in what we tell you. However, the information is certainly something you need to know, and often a lot of this information isn't passed through generations, though it should be. Our parents successfully taught us how to eat with a fork or spoon, how to keep fingers away from the nose, how to use a potty and how to say "sorry," "please" and "thank you." These basic and essential skills can either be taught to children pleasantly or as a painful chore, that is skills can also be taught unpleasantly by punishing or yelling. As with all other essential skills, reading can also be taught to children. If you show your 16-month-old child a book and he doesn't show interest, put the book away and try again later. But definitely don't accept defeat. Perseverance is critical in this situation, and though it may not be the right time right now, next time your child may just show interest. Similarly, If your child doesn't get how to write correctly the first time and ends up writing in a backward manner, don't fret. Enjoy the journey with your child. Appreciate that we all learn in different ways, at different speeds - no matter what the subject or the time in your life. Remember, we're all born ready and eager to learn [5].

2. Talk to your children a lot

There's no harm in talking to your child from her early years. Talk to her, sing to her/him about anything, talk about her/his nose, mouth, ears, fingers, and eyes. Talk to her about her/his family, dad, mom, and older siblings. You can also talk to her/him when she/he sleeps, eats, burp or yawn. Some parents tend to think that talking to a child when she's still a baby is crazy because a baby doesn't understand yet. I beg to differ; reading is a language activity and as such, to learn the language, you need to hear it before you can speak it. As a matter of fact, studies have shown that teaching by way of saying a variety of words to your young child or baby helps in the development of literacy skills. I suppose the phrase "catch them when they are young" also applies to reading. Not only that, but communicating is also done via social cues, tone of voice and body language - things that babies, infants and children are very responsive to. So, talking as well as using your body language to communicate is an effective way of spurring on their development. Many studies go one step further, suggesting the use of a silly voice is beneficial in your child picking up language [6].

3. Read to your child

I describe reading to children as the foundation of developing a solid reading skill. Reading to children is a good idea, and it helps. There are several alternatives to reading for parents who can't read English; such parents could use an audiobook but for parents who can read English, reading a story or a book to a child is an excellent idea as it helps to improve literacy skills in children. Several studies have confirmed that reading to children helps to improve their literacy skills. When you read to a child, you expose them to vocabulary that is richer than the spoken words they hear from adults who talk to them. This has a positive impact on their intelligence, language and literacy achievement as they grow. There are quite a number of beautiful books to read to children; you can visit your local library to choose from the vast array of adventure books to read to children.

Truth be told, the process of teaching your child how to read is one that starts at infancy though I do not advise that you teach your baby reading with flashcards. No. I am encouraging you to start reading with your baby a day after you welcome her into your home. Besides the fact that the time is a special bonding time for mothers and babies, it's also a perfect time to instil love for books. You need to teach your child not just to read, but to enjoy reading. Failure to teach your child to enjoy reading from an early age will most likely frustrate their efforts to enjoy reading down the road. There's no limit to the books to read to your child in a day, the number of books you read is entirely up to you. You can read at least 3-4 books a day while your child is young but as she gets older, make it a habit to read together for at least 30 minutes daily.

One study in particular details how parents play a vital role in the development of cognitive and reading skills by reading to their children from a young age. Giving us an insight that when we frequently read to children around the ages of 4 and 5, it has a significant positive effect on them all the way up to around the age of 10 or 11 [7].

Here are suggestions of books to read to your child. These are just suggestions; you can always read whatever your child enjoys.

- Birth - One year: Songbooks, Bible stories, Psalms, Lullabies, Cloth books (with different textures), Board Books (with pictures).
- One year – Three years: Songbooks, Bible stories, Psalms, Rhyming Books, Short-Story board books.
- Three years - Five Years: Song Books, Bible stories Psalms, Alphabet Books, Rhyming books and Picture Books.

4. Have your child tell you a story

Another great way to introduce children to reading is to listen to their story or take their dictation. Have them make up a story or recount their experience. Their story maybe something like, "I like grandma," "I like Chicken," "I like my brother." Write the stories as they are being told and then read aloud. While reading, make sure to point at the words as you read them or point at the words when your child is reading them. Over time, your child would be able to identify words such as "like" or "I" even without pointing at them.

Not only is this good for literacy development and communication, it also encourages creativity - when a child is crafting their own story, they are utilising their imagination and allowing it to reach new heights. In the process, they are learning a love for language and building their confidence [8].

5. Teach your child phonemic awareness.

Your young child doesn't have the ability to hear the sounds within words. She hears "dog," but she doesn't hear the sound or phonemes duh - aw- guh). To make your child a reader, you need to teach them how to learn the sounds or phonemes in words. For example, say a word and then break it down into phonemes; chair - ch-ch-ch-air. "Phonemes," which are composed of short vowels, consonants, digraphs, and long vowels are the smallest sounds in the English Language. Phonemic awareness entails learning sounds and how to manage them within a word. Digraphs are unique sounds that are made up of single letters such as sh, th, ch, etc. Phonics involves learning how to spell sounds as well as the rules that bind the English language. Though phonics is an essential component of spelling and reading, it shouldn't be made the main focus. Teaching your kid the rules of phonics will help her learn to decode and spell. At the tuition centre, we use the Pathways to Reading program as our phonics and phonemic awareness, and it sure makes learning all of the complicated spellings fun. However, we do not advise that parents use it until children are in kindergarten, first grade or year 1, that is ages 5-7.

6. Teach phonics (letter names and their sounds).

To write words or sound out words, there is a need for your child to know the letter sounds. Young children learn letter sounds in kindergarten, and parents can also teach them. All you will need is a paper and pencil, but you can also get ABC books, cards, charts, floor mats, magnet letters, and puzzles. Keep the lessons fun and brief; the lesson should be no more than 10 minutes for young children as children tend to attend to activities that interest them for 10-15 minutes without getting distracted.

7. Listen to your child read

Have your child read to you. When she starts bringing books home, have her read them to you. If she doesn't sound clear or reasonable at the first read, have her read the book all over again. You can guide her by reading the book to her first before she reads it herself. Studies have shown that doing this repeatedly helps the kids to become better readers both at home and school.

Additionally, you can structure this activity and give it the foundations to provide a robust learning framework for your child. Go through the process of allowing your child to select a book and explain the reason they chose the book. The next step of action would be to encourage them to read the book and afterwards ask them what was happening, this way you can learn of their comprehension skills. After the reading session is complete, you can have a more in-depth discussion on what the book was about and how the characters were feeling. This ensures that your child is getting the most from every opportunity they have to read [9].

8. Promote writing

While you are teaching your child how to read, make sure

to promote writing. Literacy involves writing and reading so have magazines and books available for your children. Also, it's helpful to have crayons, pencils, papers, and markers available for your child to learn how to write. You can encourage your child to write by writing short letters or notes to her. Before you know it, she will start writing letters or notes back to you.

9. Ask questions

When your child reads to you, have her retell the information or story. When your child reads a story, ask her questions. You can ask her who and what the story is about and if she shares information with you, ask her what the information is about and how it works. Reading isn't just about sounding out words; it involves thinking about the story or text and remembering the events and ideas. Do not just read to your child, ask questions. Besides encouraging your child to relate with the book being read, asking your child questions while reading to her also helps to develop her ability to fully grasp what you are reading. Your main objective when reading to your child should not just be to get your child to sound out words. Your objective should be helping your child grasp what's being read. You'd be surprised that children who can sound words and read with high fluency might find it difficult to fully grasp what they are reading. What's the point of reading when a child cannot grasp what he is reading? Ask your kid questions to be sure that she comprehends what's being read. When your child is still young, ask her questions such as, "Do you see the dog?" while pointing to the picture of the dog. Asking questions will not only improve her vocabulary, but it will also encourage interaction with the book she's reading. Once your child is around 2-3 years, ask her questions before, while reading the book and after reading the book. Show her the cover of the book before reading and ask her to predict what the book is about. While reading the book, ask her why she thinks a particular character made a choice. In a case where a character is portraying a strong emotion, identify the emotion and ask her if she has ever felt the emotion. After reading the book, ask her what happened in the book or what she learnt from the book.

10. Make reading a regular activity at your home.

Make reading a regular activity at your home, and your children will thank you for it. I recollected when I was 9 years old, my mom would make me read for 30 minutes after lunch. We went to the book collection to get books to start my new activity, and this regular activity of mine made me a lifelong reader. Set aside time for everyone to read a book with no distractions. Do not just make the time a reading time, make the time fun and enjoyable.

11. Be a good example (good reader)

Even if your child develops an interest in reading from an early age, her interest will quickly reduce if she doesn't see reading being practised in her home. Even if you are not an enthusiastic reader, make sure that your child sees you reading for a few minutes. You can read a cookbook, bible, novel or a magazine, whatever rocks your boat. The point is to show your child that everyone reads, adults inclusive. As parents, we get wrapped up with the things our children should do to be successful forgetting that children learn by example.

Various studies suggest that children will mimic the behaviours and attitudes of their parents, so it's always best to go into everything educational with an open mind, as not to deter them from participating in developing skills in that area. It can be argued that children are more likely to succeed and more easily develop their skillset when their parents have succeeded in their educational journeys too [10].

12. Identify letters in natural settings

As children approach a certain age, parents tend to force them to learn the name of letters. We buy DVDs or flashcards in a bid to teach our children the name of the letters. Then we go-ahead to drill our young child over and over just for them to learn letters. Don't do this, leave your child to be a child and grab the teachable moments as they come. The mind of children are like sponges capable of learning alphabets from drilling, but drilling isn't an effective method of teaching that produces long-term results. As your child grows, she will be curious about the letters she sees around, and she will ask questions. That's not the time to drill your child but the time to use practical applications to teach your child. I am not saying that teaching your child alphabets isn't essential, but what's more important is how you teach her. Have in mind that the ultimate goal when teaching your child how to read or write is to raise a lifelong reader who's passionate about reading and not just a child who memorized letters without any significance.

13. Include multiple domains of development

I have found that children learn what they are being taught when different areas of development or different senses are incorporated. This is why hands-on teaching is more applicable and retained by children. The moment your child shows interest in letters, you should start using natural settings to identify the letters and also implement activities that include as many senses as possible. When it comes to developing letter recognition and reading skills in children, there are a number of ways to include multiple domains of development. Through the process of cutting, glueing and creating alphabet crafts to teach your child the shape of a letter as well as the sound of the letter. Games that involve gross motor skills is an excellent way of incorporating movement. Every child loves singing and rhyming so, identify the strengths and interests of your child and incorporate activities that fit them.

If you are stuck for specific ideas then inspiration for such activities can be found by a quick search on the internet. Luckily, there are thousands of resources that can help you, many of which are very useful.

14. Classify the genre

Children around 5 years can identify the difference between reality and make-belief. I advise that you teach your child the different genres of the book while you are reading together. Though teaching your child, the different genres of the book seem like a complicated or difficult task; it's not entirely difficult. I have listed five genres of books to teach your little one. You can use "type" in the place of "genre" if the type is easier to remember.

- Nonfiction books - Real facts or stories about people, places or animals.
- Fantasy - Not real. Things or events that cannot happen in real life. Talking animals or magical events.
- Realistic fiction - A made-up story that can happen in real life since the situations and characters are believable.
- Song Books
- Alphabet Books

To classify a book into a specific type or genre, your child needs to summarize the book and remember the details of the book. Then, he has to use the book information to decide the type of genre the book falls under. While doing this, your child will be remembering the details of similar books in the same genre and thereby making connections between the books. Though this activity may take time, it's sure to pack a punch of processing and thought in your child's brain. You should know that there are some books like phonics readers which do not fall under any of the listed genres. I would advise that you carry out this exercise using quality children's literature, such books can be found in libraries. Have in mind that the ultimate goal for this exercise is to help your child understand what he's reading. When you reinforce your child to reflect on and remember the details of the book he read, you are modelling him to do what you hope he'll do independently in the nearest future.

In the research process for this book, we found one method

for teaching children the difference between non-fiction and fiction was repeatedly cropping up. This method was the poster method; providing children with posters with a short definition of each of the terms, alongside related imagery. For non-fiction, the images were all from the real world, however with the fiction poster the pictures were of cartoon-like characters or mythical animals. Further defining what is real as non-fiction and what is a fantasy as fiction [11].

15. Word Families

Simply put, word families are words that sound identically. Teaching children word families helps them identify the pattern in reading. Identifying the pattern in reading is vital as it helps children to start reading by grouping the sets of letters in a word. The first set of letters in a word is referred to as the onset while the last part is called the rime. Though there are changes to onset, work families share a similar rhyme. For instance, once your child has identified the word "pop," he will find it easy to read other words with similar rime such as hop, cop, stop, mop or top.

16. Decoding

Decoding is often described as "sounding it out." Though decoding is an element to consider when teaching your child how to read, it's not the essential element. Once your child can identify the sounds of each letter, she is ready to put words together. For instance, when you are teaching your child to pronounce short words such as cat, encourage her to pronounce individual sound /c/, /a/, /t/ before putting them together as "cat." As your child learns how to decode words with accuracy and more frequency, she will be proficient at identifying words automatically. This exercise is a tedious one, so there's a need for you to incorporate things that will make it fun.

Though we state this isn't one of the essential elements in teaching your child to read, there are sources on the internet and in academic journals that do stake significant importance on this activity in their early development of children. "Early attainment of decoding skill is essential because this early skill accurately predicts later skill in reading comprehension. There is persuasive and strong evidence that children who get off to a slow start rarely become strong readers. Early learning of the code leads to wider reading habits both in and out of school" [12].

17. Sight words

Sight words which are otherwise known as high-frequency words are common words in the English language that don't follow the rules of phonics. Thus they are difficult to sound phonetically. You have to teach your child to memorize sight words. Sight words need to be memorized for your child to become an accurate and precise reader. You do not have to start with a long list of sight words. Start teaching your child a few words at a time. Activities such as Sight Word Bingo makes learning and memorizing sight words a fun activity.

As you must have probably noticed, teaching your child how to read doesn't have a specific formula. The tips and strategies listed in this chapter are simple but effective, and they are not meant to be used as a checklist. Do not use these strategies as a checklist and think that once you have implemented all these strategies, your child will be proficient at reading. This chapter provides information to use as a guide while creating a learning environment that will foster the growth of your kid as a reader. Don't be in a rush and do not overstretch your child. While it's critical to take advantage of the early years learning time, it's more important to allow your child to be a child.

Here are some practical tips for implementing every day; these tips are a summary of the strategies discussed in this chapter. Note that all the strategies discussed in this chapter cannot be implemented on all ages, so use your discretion to determine the strategy that is best for your child.

- Develop a habit of reading to your child every day.
- Make sure you ask your child questions before, while reading and after reading.
- Be a good example, that is be a good reader yourself.
- When teaching your child letters and sounds, include as many senses as possible.
- Read different varieties of book and ask your child to guess the genre.
- Make rhyming a fun activity.
- Teach your child to pronounce short words.
- Practice memorizing sight words every day and most importantly, have fun reading together with your child.

YOUR FREE GIFT!

As a way of saying thank your for
purchasing this book, I am
offer offering you a free
parenting book!

You can click on the link
below or you can wait until
the end of the book to collect
and download your free
copy.

[DOWNLOAD YOUR FREE COPY HERE](#)

2

HOW TO IMPROVE THE SPELLING ABILITIES OF YOUR CHILD

The role of a mother or father in helping children to read, write and spell is vital. No doubt, children who are good spellers are better readers.

Here are some fun and helpful ways to improve your child's spelling.

18. Play the spelling word memory game

Create two sets of word cards and play the spelling word memory game by spreading the cards so they face down and then take turns to flip two cards at once to find a pair. Though it may not seem particularly challenging, it means that the children are being exposed to a repeated set list of words. This way, the point is being hammered home of what those particular words look like, how to decode them and how to spell them. It's also an entertaining game for children where they can learn outside of the traditional classroom environment and experience.

19. Play the flip four steps game

This game allows your child to practice reading, spelling and writing down words. Have your child turn over a word card, identify the word, pronounce the word, say the letters, turn the card over and write down the word on a paper.

20. Read, read, read

The more the kids read, the more they will start memorizing the spelling of words. Keep in mind that picture books contain more simple words than early reader books, so do not replace picture books with more educational books. Instead you should move onto more educational/further developed reading materials only when your child is ready to do so.

Expanding on their knowledge, tastes and vocabulary skills is crucial to ensuring your child becomes a keen reader, effective communicator and continues to improve their concentration levels [13].

21. Practice spelling

Make spelling practise a regular activity. Keep in mind that spelling isn't an activity you teach a child once and then move on to do something else. Spelling requires review and regular practice.

22. Carry out projects that involve words

Get busy with projects that involve words. Make word collages where you cut words from a book or magazine, attach them to a paper with glue and then write down filler words to form a story.

23. Play word games

Boggle, hangman and scrabble are fun and excellent games for improving spelling. Playing a word game with your child is an easy and exciting way to learn complicated words quickly.

24. Spell and eat

While preparing breakfast, brunch, or lunch, have your child spell a word and reward her with a treat when the word is correctly spelt.

25. Surround your child with printed cards

Label the cupboard and desk of your child with printed cards showing different words to make it easy for her to learn the words every day.

26. Consider Rewarding, not punishment

Ensure to reward your child with stickers, praise, points, treats, and the like. Using positive reinforcement motivates your child to memorize more words than punishing your child when a word is wrongly spelt.

You need to understand that teaching your child to spell words at home requires patience and also demands a non-school setting. Do not try to be a teacher or a parent who commands, instead be a parent who teaches. Keep the spelling activities fun, short and do them regularly.

27. Trace, copy and recall

Fold three columns on a paper and label the first column "trace," label the second column "copy," and the third column "recall". Write the word in the first column labelled trace and have your child trace the letters. Have her copy the word to the second column and finally, hide the first two columns and have her remember the spelling of the word and write it down without guidance.

Fun and exciting spelling games using a pen, pencil, marker and paper

28. Spelling Word Race

Form two teams and have each team take a turn holding the pen. Prepare a list of words and call out a word for the players on the team to write down the word quickly.

Not only does this make things more exciting and fun for your child, it also adds a competitive element to something which may have previously seemed like a relatively dull task.

29. Spelling Puzzle

Create a homemade puzzle by writing words in large letters on an index card. Have your kid cut out each word and then try to put the puzzle back together.

30. Stair steps

Write down words and arrange them like they are stairs, adding a letter one after the other.

- *S*
- *St*
- *Sta*
- *Stai*
- *Stair*

31. Tic-Tac-Toe

Create a large-sized board and play tic-tac-toe. Have each player write down a spelling word. Also, this game can be played in a different way. Have each player use an 'O' or 'X', but to place a mark on the board, each player is required to spell a word correctly.

32. Window Writing

Use unique window safe crayons. Window writing makes learning word spelling fun and exciting. Window safe crayons can be found from various outlets on the high street and retailers on the internet. They are relatively affordable and are great for helping your little one on his/her literacy journey.

33. Flip and Rainbow Write

Flip a word card over and have the child write and paint each flipped word in rainbow colours. The first word should be coloured red, the second-word orange and the third word should be coloured yellow.

34. Water Paint

Using water and a paintbrush, have your child identify words and paint spelling words.

Fun and exciting ways to learn word spelling using a computer and other fun electronics

35. Type it out

Open a word document on a computer. Call spelling words loudly and have your child type the words on the screen. Enlarge the font of the text and make it a cool colour.

36. Spell on Tape

Set the voice recorder on the computer or on your phone and have your child spell words correctly.

37. Video Record

Make a video of your child spelling words. Have her dress up, wear a silly hat or use a silly prop to make the activity more exciting.

38. Karaoke

That karaoke machine can be used as a fun spelling machine. Simply turn it on and have your child spell his words into it.

Though it's not your traditional night of karaoke, it does give your child the spotlight, making them feel louder and more noticeable than before. This is therefore a definite confidence booster.

39. Use Puzzlemaker

Let your child type in all her spelling words and then search for them with the puzzle maker.

40. Use Let them sing it

Let Them Sing It is a site that turns spelling words into a song. Have your child spell words on this site and the word is sung back to your child.

41. Use Spelling City

Spelling City is a site which allows your child to type in his spelling words, learn the words, play games with the words and then take a test.

Fun and exciting ways to learn word spelling using space to run, jump, and play:

42. Chalkboard Race

Form two teams and have a player from each team hold a piece of chalk and stand at a spot away from the chalkboard. Call out a word and have the players run to the board to write the correct spelling. The player who writes the correct spelling first is the winner.

43. Ball Toss

Children form a circle with a ball or with a safe object to pass around. Call out a word then pass the ball to a child, and the child spells the word. If the word is misspelt, the child passes the ball to the next person to spell the word. If the child correctly spells the word, he passes the ball to the next child and the teacher or parent calls out a new word to spell.

44. Swing and Spell

The parent or teacher calls out a word for a child to spell and he spells the word with each back and forth manoeuvres of the swing.

45. Run the Bases

The game starts with the child at a home plate. The parent or teacher calls out a word to spell and the child moves around the base starting with hitting the ball, running from the first base to the second and third base and back to the home plate while spelling the word.

Fun and exciting ways to learn word spelling with anything and everything else

46. Spelling Word Hunt

Have your child circle or highlight the spelling words listed at the back of a newspaper, in a book, text or a magazine.

47. Crazy Words:

Pour body cream, rice or sand on a cookie sheet and have your child write spelling words on the tray with his fingers.

48. Paint bag Writing

Pour poster paint in a gallon-sized Ziploc bag and close it tightly. Have your child write the letters of each word on the paint bag with her fingertips.

49. Stamp It

With the aid of an alphabet letter stamp, have your child stamp spelling words by first looking at the words and writing them with no guidance.

Fun and exciting games to learn word spelling with magnetic letters or letter cards:

50. Word Scramble

Rearrange the letters of each word and have your child arrange them in the right order. Make sure to point out families and patterns.

51. Word Train

Have your child form a word train by forming a new word with the last letter of the first word. For example, tap - pan - net.

52. Examine the Word

Pick a spelling word, look at the word closely and talk to your child about the tough parts of the word. Teach your child silly ways to remember the tough parts of a spelling word. For example, 'chocolate' has an 'o' in the middle because chocolate is sweet.

Creativity

Probably the most crucial aspect in a child's educational journey to literacy competence and success is opening their mind to new ideas, innovative thinking and breaking the mould. When your child first begins to read, there will be many new ideas presented to them. Whether it's a talking dog - something we would consider very out of the ordinary as it is entirely unrealistic, or whether it's an astronaut going to space - something very realistic but bizarre to somebody who doesn't know anything outside of their own home, school and town.

Embracing your child's creativity, encouraging them to think in the same way as the writers whose pieces of fiction they are reading can be hugely beneficial. As we have already mentioned, you should be encouraging your child to tell stories and get their brain working creatively, but also open their mind up to as many new situations as possible. Ensure they know astronauts are real, ensure they know dogs can't really talk - but most importantly, ensure they know that anything can happen in a book and that the world is their oyster. Make it fun, keep it educational and keep their attention in the process.

You can achieve this through first educating them on it, then by inviting them to tell you a bedtime story, or write something new.

A friend once told me that she encouraged her son to write her a story and what she read was incredible. It was a blend of characters he had seen on television, they joined forces and went on to stop a bad guy who had a very evil plan. Though his characters weren't anything new, there was a clear narrative, fantastical elements and the themes were heavily focused on friendship and teamwork. It was clear that her child had effectively utilised his literacy skills to form his own story. He was combining theory with practicality and forming new ideas that would have stayed dormant in his mind otherwise.

3

SIMPLE STRATEGIES FOR TEACHING YOUR CHILD MATHEMATICS AT HOME

Teaching your child mathematics at home is as easy as adding 1+1 = 2. There are a number of methods to teach your child mathematics at home without having a pencil and paper. It's essential for your child to understand mathematics. Good knowledge of math is needed to get your child through her study years. Math is applicable both outside and inside the school. Truth be told, math can be somewhat dull and challenging for kids, but with a little teaching at home, maths can quickly become an exciting subject. You can help make mathematics an intriguing subject for your child by taking away the seriousness of math and turning the subject into a fun and creative activity.

Particularly when your children reaches the age of 11 all the way up to the age of 16, you'll likely notice that they seem disengaged with learning. This is as a result of the sheer number of distractions in their social lives between those ages.

Between their social lives and wanting to get invited to all the outings, they don't really have much time or attention for learning - and even when they are doing it, their minds are often elsewhere. Whether it's English or Mathematics, children between the ages of 11 and 16 probably find their teachers boring, the subjects dull and in the case of Mathematics, it can seem difficult to see how relevant the subject will be in later life.

Particularly in the case of algebra, it's so easy for a child between the ages of 11 and 16 to completely disregard the topic as irrelevant, pointless and ultimately, a waste of time. So, it's essential to engage your child in Mathematics based activities at home too, probably more-so than literacy-based activities.

This chapter discusses the quick and easy strategies to teach children mathematics at home and turn them into young mathematicians.

53. Begin with counting

When it comes to mathematics, numbers are significant. Teaching mathematics starts with your child identifying her numbers. You can teach your kid how to count with the same strategies you will employ to teach her mathematics. You can have her memorize numbers as you call them or have her pick up numbers by counting objects from 1-10. You need to understand that the method that works for one child may work or not work for the other child. Once your child has learnt how to count, you can start teaching her some simple math principles and before you know it, she will be subtracting and adding.

54. Use Everyday Objects

You have everything needed to teach your child mathematics at home. You have enough objects at your disposal; pennies, buttons, cars, books, money, soup cans, fruits, and trees. Mathematics is easy to teach a child when you have physical objects at your disposal to count, subtract, add and multiply. Everyday objects also teach children that objects need not be identical before they can be used in mathematics. Teaching your child to count mangoes is a great lesson but you'd agree with me that counting oranges, apples, watermelons and mangoes helps to expand his thought process. He's counting various objects instead of counting routine numbers 1-10.

55. Play Math Games

There are games in the market to help teach your child mathematics. For example, adding dice and Hi Ho Cherry-O teaches simple addition while Ladders and Chutes will introduce your child to numbers 1-100. Classic games such as Monopoly, Life, PayDay and Yahtzee are excellent tools for addition and subtraction. You can also create a math game from your imagination. Have your child play a math scavenger hunt. Write a number on the driveway with chalk, ask your child fundamental math question and have him answer by running to the correct number on the driveway. Whatever the math game you choose, make sure the game will make your child enjoy mathematics rather than see mathematics as an educational drill.

56. Bake Cookies

A soft cookie is an excellent resource for teaching mathematics. While your child can count cookies, you can also teach your child fractions using a fresh batch of cookies. Teach your kids how to cut a cookie into halves, fourths or eighths with a plastic knife. Making fractions from a whole visually leaves an impression in your child's mind. Use small cookie pieces to teach your child how to add and subtract fraction. For instance, with small cookie pieces, show your child that two halves of a small cookie make a whole cookie (1/2 of a cookie + 1/2 of a cookie = 1 whole cookie). You also can make your playdough or use raw cookie dough as an alternative to baking cookies. Your child cannot eat raw cookie fractions after learning maths, but you can keep the cookie dough to reuse for the math lesson.

57. Invest in Abacus or traditional tools

You do not need to download a fancy app on your laptop to teach your child mathematics at home. Instead, use traditional math toys like an abacus. An abacus helps to teach children math skills starting from counting to addition and subtraction. An abacus is reliable as it doesn't run down on battery power or break like a toy laptop.

An abacus is a useful and excellent resource for teaching kids' addition, multiplication, subtraction and division. Even the smallest hands enjoy playing with an abacus. Besides teaching your child basic subtraction, addition, multiplication or division, an abacus also helps to develop problem-solving skills in children.

58. Test Flash Cards

Though flashcards can show the addition of two numbers, letting children do the counting themselves work better. Take a step further by evaluating the learning preferences of your child by trying both manual counting and flash cards. While some children learn mathematics better by counting pictures on a card, others learn by seeing the answer to a sum on a card. Others will not get the concept fully until they count physical objects. Try out different methods to be sure of the method that works best for your child.

59. Make Math a Daily Activity

Incorporate mathematics into the daily routine of your child. Help your child benefit from math lesson by incorporating it in his daily life and at the same time, make sure to set goals that they can achieve in a lesson.

60. Show your child that mathematics is fun

Ask your child basic and simple mathematics questions in a fun and exciting way.

Ask questions such as:

- How many black cars do you see at a red light?
- How many boxes of crackers can we buy with £10 at the grocery store?
- When you go to the doctor's office, ask your child the number of the kids that will be left in the waiting room after three kids have been attended to.
- While having lunch, ask your child the amount of food you would have left if you only ate 1/4 of the food.
- While driving on the freeway, ask your child to add

up the numbers on the license plate of the vehicle driving in front of your car.
- Ask your child how much diapers cost if there's a discount of 25%.
- How many trousers are you putting into the washing machine?
- If you are asked to share eight quarters between four people, how many quarters would you give each person?

Once you show your child that math can be fun and exciting, she will be passionate about learning mathematics. Once your child is passionate about learning, there's no stopping for him.

61. Number everything

Start numbering everything right from the early years of your child. Count his fingers and toes while changing his diaper. Count the segments of mandarin you give him, count the oranges you place in a bag at the grocery store. The idea is to take advantage of any opportunity that allows your child to count. When you start teaching your child how to count from his early years, you can be rest assured that he will know his numbers by the time he's ready for pre-school.

62. The TV can be educational

If you do not allow your children to watch TV programs, break the rule and allow them to watch Sesame Street. Sesame Street is a children TV series that teaches children cognitive skills, including mathematics. Mickey Mouse Clubhouse and

Numbers around the Globe are both TV programs that teach young children how to count.

63. Make math a game

Learning is always fun when it's made into a game. Here are a few fun games to help teach your child math at home.

Set the table

Have your child set the table for a specific amount of people with unbreakable crockery and cutlery. As he sets the cups and plates, count the numbers loudly and encourage him to repeat after you.

64. Size comparison

Instruct your child to arrange his toy dinosaurs or toy cars from the smallest to the biggest. Pick two toys of different sizes and ask him to identify the smaller and bigger size.

65. Patterns

Lego and other blocks are a great resource to form patterns with. You can also form patterns with shape or colour.

66. Incorporate the lingo

Make sure to incorporate math concept words when discussing everyday things with your child. Use words such as "a few", "a lot," or "some". The words won't be new or strange to him when he has to use the words in the classroom.

67. Shapes

Introduce your child to shapes by identifying or naming the shapes you see in the garden or in the house.

68. Junior Monopoly

While junior monopoly is appropriate for older kids, it can

be used to teach children math skills through the paper cash and it can also serve as a way of bonding the family.

69. Piggybank

A piggy bank is an excellent way to teach your child mathematics and the importance of saving. With the coins in a piggy bank, you can teach your child counting, subtraction or addition. If you are using a piggy bank to teach younger children math, make sure to count the coin loudly as they drop in the till. Older children can learn addition by adding up the money they have collected. They can also learn subtraction by removing a certain amount from the money to buy something.

70. BBC Bitesize

There are many potential outlets for supporting the framework your child is being taught at school in their Mathematics lessons (and English too). One option available to you is BBC Bitesize. This platform is excellent for fun, educational, informative and challenging activities for your children, no matter what exam they are preparing for. Mostly focusing on Mathematics, English and key subjects, this can be a fresh approach to learning that incorporates digital technology in a more positive way.

For one mother, her son was completely uninterested in maths, so much so that he was flunking. The mother decided to employ some of these strategies in an attempt to work together to overcome this. These tips were critical in not only overcoming his lack of enthusiasm, but also the fear that had grown from constantly doing poorly and being berated immediately afterwards. She said that it was extremely crucial for her to switch her tactics and get involved with her son's education. At first, he was unwilling to cooperate, but she decided to make a game out of maths and take a slower paced approach at home. They advanced from simple math games while like setting the table and recognizing patterns, to eventually more formal study with his textbook and workbook. She said that there was definitely no quick solution and they tried a number of things with her son, some of which worked and some of which weren't as successful. It took time to develop good study habits with her son. However, she recognized that she first had to work on her relationship with her son to understand why he was uninterested and validate his fears before proceeding with the different strategies presented in this chapter in order to get her son reacquainted with maths.

4

TEACHING YOUR KIDS ENGLISH AT HOME

Why Should Children be Taught English at an Early Stage?

If I asked you how you learnt and became fluent in your mother tongue, what would your answer be? I'm sure you'd tell me that you are fluent in your language because you started learning it since you were a child. You should also teach your child English in a similar manner so that your child can gain enough practice and be fluent.

What are the Benefits of teaching your child English from an early age?

- It makes the child more exposed.
- It helps children develop a habit of communicating in English.
- Learning a foreign language offers cognitive benefits such as enhanced memory, problem-

solving skills, increased creativity, the flexibility of mind and network critical thinking.
- Cultural enrichment
- Better access to information on the internet
- Higher academic achievement.

A lot of parents want to teach English to their kids at home but they are unsure of how and where to start. Teaching English to your child at home doesn't require you to be perfect or have a degree in the English language. The essential thing is that you are zealous and you encourage your children. Do not fret or worry when and if your child doesn't speak the language immediately, your child will need some time to learn the language. Teach them and be patient with them and you will find that they will speak the language in their own time.

Children learn a new language easily and quickly at a prime age. If you want your child to be well versed in spoken English, then start teaching him at an early age. Take advantage of the early teaching years and immerse your child in English language. Ensure that you incorporate spoken English into your child's daily routine to facilitate an extensive vocabulary.

Here are some ways to teach your child English language at home.

71. Establish a routine

Create time for English lessons at home. It's better to have short but frequent sessions than having long and not frequent sessions. Fifteen minutes is enough to teach your young child the English language on a daily basis. As your child gets older, you can gradually make the session longer. Make sure to keep the activities varied and short in a bid to grab the attention of your child. Make sure to carry out certain activities at the same time on a daily basis. Children feel more confident and comfortable when they can predict what to expect. For example, you can develop a routine of reading an English story to your child before bedtime or playing an English game after school every day. If your home is spacious, you can create an English space to keep things that are related to English such as games, books or DVDs. Keep in mind that repetition is necessary as children want to hear phrases or words before they can produce them on their own.

72. Playing games

Studies have shown that children learn when the activity is fun and exciting. Flashcard is a great way to teach children vocabulary and there are several games you can play alongside flashcards. They include; Happy Families, Kim's game, Snap or Memory. Also, there are several other games to play with your child to help her learn English.

- Board games - Snakes and ladders and other traditional games
- Action games - What's the time Mr. Wolf? Charades and Simon says.
- Word games - Hangman, I spy.

73. Using everyday situations

The advantage of teaching your child English at home is

that you can use real objects and everyday situations to learn and practice the language in context and naturally.

For example:

- Talk to your child about clothes when you are arranging laundry or when your child is getting dressed.
- Teach your child vocabulary for furniture and toys when you are tidying up the room.
- Teach your child food vocabulary when you are shopping at the grocery store or when you are cooking. When next you go to the supermarket or a store, give your child the list of groceries to find. When you get home, revise the vocabulary as you are putting the groceries in the appropriate places.

74. Using stories

Young children are attracted to books with attractive illustrations and bright colours. Identify the pictures together and pronounce the words as you identify the pictures. After reading, you can ask your child to point to different pictures. For example, ask your child to point to the picture of a cat. Also, encourage learning by asking him to pronounce the words. Reading stories to your child will get him familiar with the rhythms and sounds of English.

75. Using songs

A song is an effective way to teach children pronunciations and new words. Songs that are actionable are suitable for young children since they can demonstrate even if they are unable to sing the song. Your child can use hand gestures to demonstrate the meaning of the words mentioned in the song. Schools should resist putting additional time and resources into yet more English and maths lessons and instead give children's learning a research-evidenced boost by encouraging them to join a band or an orchestra, says **Martin Leigh**.

76. Teaching grammar

When teaching young children English language at home, you need not teach grammar rules explicitly. Instead, make sure that they are used to hearing and using grammatical structures in different contexts. For example, 'must or mustn't', when you are talking about home or school rules and 'have got' when you are talking about the appearance of a person. Learning how grammatical structures are used in different contexts from an early age goes a long way in helping your child to apply it correctly and naturally when they grow older. When your young child grows older, she can in turn teach her siblings or friends how to use grammatical structures in different contexts. While your older child is teaching others how to use grammar, she is also teaching herself further.

77. Which phrases and words should I teach first?

Consider the personality and interest of your child when deciding the topics to teach your child. Also, you can ask your child to help you select the topics to teach. You may start teaching with some of these topics:

- Numbers (1–10; 10–20; 20–100).

- Adjectives (e.g. big, small, tall, happy, sad, tired).
- Colours
- Part of the body
- toys
- clothes
- animals (e.g. pets, farm animals, wild animals)
- food

It's vital that you use the same phrase with your child every time so your child can get familiar with English Time language. Use phrases such as "It's English time" "Shall we sit down", "which book or story should we start with today?" Over time, your child will pick up phrases such as thank you, please, identify, where is? point to, it's, I don't like, I like, what's the name of?, what colour is it?

Regardless of the approach you use, the most important thing is to make English time a relaxing fun and enjoyable time for you and your child.

78. Have 'English only' days in your home

All children enjoy playing games, most especially games that bring about a friendly competition between siblings. Set aside a day in the week to be an 'English only' day in your home. This means that English is the only allowed language on English only days. Set aside a small jar and place in a conspicuous area such as kitchen counter for anyone who speaks a language that is different to English language to drop a marble. At the end of the day, count the number of marbles in the jar and declare the child with the least amount of marvels the winner of the competition.

79. Play 'rainy day' games

Rainy day games are referred to as the easy and quick games you can play without using many materials. A perfect example of such a game is Hangman. Hangman is a quick and easy game that will get your child to spell and communicate in English. The materials needed to play hangman are simply a pencil and paper. Another activity that encourages English speaking is creating a story. Creating a story is ideal for a small group. You will have each child write her name at the top right corner of a piece of paper with the title "once upon a time". Have each child pass their paper to the next person on the left. Each child will write the first sentence of the story, fold the paper and pass to the next person. Make sure that the children do not see the written first sentences. Have them write the second sentence of the story, fold the paper and then pass to the next person. The cycle continues until the papers get to the original owners. After each child must have completed the story, have them read the story aloud. Children enjoy playing this game, as such, they will want to play again and again. It's a fun and creative way to teach your children spoken English without living the comfort of your living room.

80. Watch a movie in English

Let technology and media work to your advantage. Give your child the opportunity to choose a movie to watch in English. Pause the movie occasionally to ask questions such as, "Why do you think a particular character said a statement"

"How do you think the movie is going to end?" At the end of the movie, ask your child his favourite part and his least favourite part and have him answer in English. Further to teaching children to speak English, watching movies in English also introduces children to a wide variety of vocabulary contexts, phrases and words. Also, English movies help to internalise the right English pronunciation in children. Set aside a night to watch an English movie in a week. Watch English movie with your child the same night every week. To make it more fun and exciting, have the child who wins the English only day to choose the English movie to watch on English movie nights. These fun activities will encourage your children to speak English fluently.

81. Hire an English speaking nanny/babysitter

Hire an English speaking nanny/babysitter to teach your child on nights when you need to work shifts or leave your children at home. Both your child and you will benefit from hiring an English speaking nanny/babysitter. How? You will be at ease wherever you know that your child is having an exciting and educational evening. A child's nanny/babysitter is someone who takes care of children when the parents or other members of the family are not available. They care for the basic needs of children such as feeding and bathing. They also organise activities that will allow children to learn more about the world and identify their interests. Unlike parents or siblings, English language may be the only language that a nanny/babysitter understands. This will drive your children to put more efforts into speaking English in a bid to communicate fluently with the caregiver. While your child is gradually making efforts to communicate with the nanny/babysitter, she is also improving her English speaking abilities.

82. Play online educational computer games

There are quite a number of free educational games to help teach children English Language. These educational games are useful tools or resources to teach children spoken English. Many of such games speak to your child in English, thus teaching him words pronunciation. These games speak to your child and show him pictures at the same time. This method of teaching provides context and also repeat words thereby helping your child pronounce the repeated words correctly. These educational games are perfect for children who are just learning vocabulary, new to vocabulary or not familiar with in-depth vocabulary. After entertaining with a game a few times, your children will have a better understanding of what a myriad of vocabulary words relate to, although he might not know the meaning of the words.

When you teach your child spoken English using the discussed methods, you can be rest assured that your child will learn to speak English without thinking. Don't just practice these methods and stop. After trying these activities or methods, ask your child for the activities they enjoyed and the ones they didn't enjoy. Do not be discouraged and don't stop teaching. A little English practise every day will combine to give your child a head start needed to master the English language later on.

5

HOMEWORK & STUDY SKILLS

How to assist your child in developing good study habits

Good study habits are not inbuilt in a child, they are learnt. As a parent, creating a daily and weekly plan for your child can help him have an understanding of what she needs to study. Likewise, giving your child rewards for every task she accomplishes can help her study hard and effectively since she is aware that there's a beautiful reward at the end of it. Good study habits do not come to a child naturally or easily, children needs to be taught good study habits to develop them. This can be hard for a parent who is unsure of how to get involved in a child's homework.

It's expedient for parents to learn effective study strategies as it helps to reduce the stress children face at school and also improve their grades. Efficient study strategies can also come in handy while your child is doing homework to avoid struggles.

Your child needs to know that there is more to studying than just sitting down to revise notes. You need to teach your child that studying entails knowing what to study, the time to study and keeping track of tests and assignments.

A number of teachers list daily assignments as well as due dates. Your kid can use this to plan his study time. Here are some tips you can teach your child to develop good study habits.

83. Create a calendar

Teach your child how to use the calendar to track assignments; teach your child how to mark dates on calendars with a marker to keep track of assignments. She can mark dates with due dates for appointments, activities and assignments on a calendar with different coloured markers. Also, you can teach your child how to use online calendar sync with his laptop or smartphone.

84. Create a weekly planner

Teach your kids how to use a calendar to prepare a study plan for the week. With a calendar, show your child how to transfer her obligations from a calendar to a weekly planner, ensuring that he includes time to work on the assignments before the due dates. You can also teach her to download a weekly list from her online calendar.

85. Create a daily checklist.

Though creating a checklist may seem like a daunting task, creating a checklist from the weekly plan is very helpful. The daily checklist or daily to-do-list will help your child to keep track of his daily activities and also see the progress she's making. Encourage your child to list her daily tasks in the order of importance and she should do the task accordingly.

86. "CHECK" into studying.

Once your child has figured out what to study, the next step is to learn how to study. Learning how to study can be broken down into a "CHECK" list with each letter standing for a step in the process of learning how to study.

87. Consider location.

What location works best for your child? Is it the library, at home or the tuition centre? While some teens work better without distractions, other teens like to have someone with them just in case they need help. Make an effort so that your child studies or does his homework in the location he chooses.

88. Have all materials handy

Looking for a calculator or a pencil when studying can cause a distraction. As such, it's your duty to help your child set aside a place to keep his homework materials so they are always available to use once she starts studying.

89. Establish rewards.

Establish rewards to motivate your child when she's studying. For instance, for every chapter she reads, you might allow her to use the computer for 15 minutes. When you make giving rewards a habit, she will eventually learn how to reward herself. She could snack between algebra and English homework.

90. Create a study checklist.

A study checklist includes all the steps your child needs to follow to study daily and to do her homework. A study checklist lists all the steps and this makes it easier for her to get started on her task and also manage her time. Likewise, a study checklist will make her homework seem less daunting than it is.

91. Keep a worry pad.

A worry pad is a tool designed for children who are easily carried away by their own thoughts. Rather than get carried away with the distracting things that pop into her head, instead she should write them on the worry pad to deal with them later after she's done studying.

92. Know the teachers

Relate to your child's teachers. Attend school events like parent evenings to sit and socialise with your child's teachers. Ask questions about their homework and how you can get involved.

93. Make your home a homework-friendly environment

Ensure that your home is friendly enough for your child to write and complete her homework. Also, keep supplies such as pencils, scissors, papers and glue within reach.

94. Reduce distractions

Reduce distractions such as loud music, phone calls or TV. Though a phone call to a classmate asking about an assignment is helpful.

95. Ensure that your kids do their homework on their own

Your child will not learn if he doesn't think for himself and make mistakes. Make yourself available to direct your child and make suggestions. You need to understand that it's the duty of your child to do the learning.

96. Be a monitor and a motivator

Ask your child about tests, quizzes and assignments. Make sure to check completed homework, encourage your child and be available to answer questions.

97. Lead by example

Has your child ever seen you reading a book or balancing your budget? Studies have shown that children follow the examples of their parents more than the advice they give.

98. Praise their work and efforts.

Praise the work and efforts of your child. Post an aced project or test on the refrigerator for every member of the family to see. Mention your child's academic achievement to friends and relatives.

99. Encourage your child to think positively

Encourage your kid to have a positive mindset towards studying as a positive mindset make a difference. Help your child change negative statements such as "I will never get a good grade in this subject" to "I started studying later than expected and I'm convinced that I'll get a good grade in the exam."

100. Teach your child active reading

It's easy for your child to skim through a book chapter without having an idea of what the chapter is all about. Teach your child active reading by encouraging her to note down the main idea of a chapter and also search for the meaning of unfamiliar concepts or words.

Steve is a young boy who reads through text books in minutes, once he told his mum that he has got the gist of the book as he drops it but mum notices that he has not applied the knowledge so mum was being thorough with him as she helped him with it by reading through each line, this is essential here. He was able to jot down the points and when he finished this, he was asked to close his book and try to remember all that he can remember from what he had read. He was not able to remember much, so mum made him repeat the process again and again deliberately and he was now able to remember, practically all that he had read. This lesson not only helped him for the immediate but also became an habits as he did that more, he began to change in his understanding and comprehending what is being read. He does his reading after supper each day and before the mum knew it she had had trained the child to have appetite for reading which has stayed with him. He also stopped reading and snacking as an habit he had formed which made him to lack concentration while reading.

101. Review the strategies for taking a test

It's natural for your child to feel stressed days or hours before taking a test or an exam. However, there are some strategies you can teach your child to help her deal with stress and be at her best during the exam. First, ensure that your child gets settled on time for the exam and is well relaxed. Encourage her to read all the instructions on the test or exam paper so she doesn't feel rushed.

There was a story of a boy called Stanley, who was well prepared for his 11plus exam, an exam taken by 11 years old in year 6 in the United Kingdom to get into the grammar school. Stanley had worked hard and practised all the past questions available as at the time, so when he got into the exam hall, he quickly saw that the comprehension and verbal reasoning that he was to answer was one of the exact past papers he had practised with mum at home, as he started answering the questions he was so relaxed knowing that he would do well but he was not sure of an instruction on the paper and he asked the invigilator who wrongly advised him not to do that part of the paper and he had initially consented to the invigilator but just a few minutes before the exam was to be over he remembered that his tuition centre teacher had told him to go through written instruction carefully and do what he has understood from it, this made him now to start having a go at the questions.

Doing home work with them also helps prepare them for test and exams so that they do not cheat in exams or test.

A child once told the parents not to come for her parents evening to get the feedback of her yearly report because she did badly. Her parents were so much concerned that she gets good result in all her subjects in class and she was just not getting it that way in exam, this made her both parents always on her case, so to relieve herself from them she told her best friend in class so that one helps her by allowing her to cheat or copy her work during class test but when it came to final exam she could not have a go to do well and meet the parents expectations, so she decided that they don't come for her final parent's evening but they did and discovered all that has been going on, the parents initially went to school to defend their child's behaviour, but they saw for themselves, what some children are in school is completely different to what they are at home and most teachers will give an honest view of what they have seen there in school and not what is not seen.

So they helped her to start preparing for the exams even after all the preparation she still failed, but this was still good because it reveals what a great gap that was missing and they try to accept her and work with her till she was still able to get the expected grades.

The parents got good counsel which was now able to constrain their child in a particular path of which helped to train her deliberately. It is not good to put pressure on children for grades. Some children cheat because they are scared of getting bad result, so since parent value education more than anything, they cheat and make parents happy.

Do you wonder how a low ability boy who played PlayStation all through the weekend got 100% in an end of term Maths assessment, they played smart. This is the time to train children to be deligent at their work but he that must teach diligence must also be diligent.

The early years of a child's life is usually formed by mums so a child that is left alone will bring the mother shame. Steve mum remembers this all the time from the grand mother. The mum changed her job to be more available for her, she will ask her daily about what she has done at school and be interested in it.

If her child is reading a book at school, she will read the book ahead to get ready to answer the questions of the child. She was not an expert in the subject but just enough to be able to help her child.

When she comes across a topic she did not understand then she will call a tutor to teach the child that topic and print out question on the topic to verify that the topic is well understood by the child, or better still she will ask her friend or tutor to teach her and once she gets it she then transfers the knowledge to her child, most young children prefer to be taught by mums.

She did not have to know all the subject but she was just interested with her child's learning, just that simple interest will help your child willing to learn. If you get a tutor watch what is being done, so sad to say that Mrs Jones employed teachers for her son but she was never there to ensure that teaching was taking place, guess what was happening before, child was only gisting with the tutor for a paid one hour lesson, it is not enough to get a teacher you must follow through what is being taught as well.

Misbehaving in school can seriously be traced to a lot of the missing links from home even though a lot of people will like to blame school system for everything, parents have a major part to play. They had thought that they will have ready all by just taking the child to school but it does not work that way, we all have to learn to give clear instruction, correction and modelling.

102. Enrol your child in a tuition Center to fill learning gaps

Enrolling your child in tuition also helps to improve his learning. At T.C.E.C, we have helped thousands of students understand what they were taught in class but didn't understand. Some students do not understand what they are taught in class; this could be as a result of disruption or distraction, absence in class, sickness, failure to understand the concept, missed classes or not having a permanent teacher. These are a few reasons why students fall back in learning and need to fill lesson gaps. Learning gaps develop in students for many reasons, hence the urgent need to fill the gap and good learning centres do an excellent job in this. Most teens, most notably the girls choose when to listen to teachers, and many of them do not listen because they do not like the teacher. This is one of the many reasons why parents enrol children at tuition centres so they can learn missed principles. It's crucial that you ask your child if she's happy with the teacher, otherwise she won't pay attention or listen to the teacher and go about daydreaming. Once your child is happy with the teacher, she will pay attention and concentrate and then be able to understand the topics.

While some children like to do homework and get more sheets of homework to consolidate learning through repetition, others do not insist on homework and do not like repetition. As such, it's essential for parents to understand that children are different and what works for A will not work for B. It's up to professional teachers to do what is right by accurately assessing the need of a child and working out a plan that will help the child achieve predicted grades.

103. My Maths, BBC Bitesize and More

As mentioned previously, platforms like BBC Bitesize can be very beneficial to supporting your child's learning when they are at home. Particularly when they are studying for an exam, this can reinforce critical areas of knowledge where they feel they may be hazy. My Maths is purely focused on Mathematics but presents games in an entertaining way, using some very well known IPs too, for instance Deal or No Deal and Countdown.

One mother told me how her sons and daughters religiously used My Maths, physics and chemistry tutor .com (for past exam questions with work through answers) and BBC Bitesize when they were in secondary school and the resources that were on the sites had a significantly positive effect on their exam preparation. Allowing them to fill in the missing gaps in their knowledge and put them at ease before they went into the exam hall for what would have otherwise been a very stressful experience.

104. Combating Negative Behaviour

Especially when your child is at home, this is when they'll express the most negativity about school and learning. It's essential to squash those thoughts and feelings as early as you can and ensure they stay on track in their educational journeys.

It's so easy for your child to speak negatively about school, homework and learning and then choose to spend the rest of their night on technology - whether it's social media on their mobile phones or getting a couple of hours of gaming on the Xbox One. It's important where possible to discourage this though and attempt to encourage them to continue learning and expanding their knowledge base.

There are various ways you can attempt to do this; one of which is by attempting to show them that you are as passionate about their learning experience as they should be, and therefore it's not just learning, it's bonding time too.

If your child sees learning as a time to bond with their parents too, they may see it in a more positive way, especially if you can find a way of presenting the information in a more exciting and fun way than their teachers could have. Another reason they may be more inclined to learn this way at home maybe if you see it as way more informal than the traditional classroom setting - appear chilled out about it and they will similarly act in the same manner. Make learning at home into something it usually isn't - make it fun, relaxed, natural and where possible, entertaining.

It's going to be so easy for your child to reach for the Xbox One controller when they get home from school, but show them that distractions will not benefit them in later life. Though, this can't always be the case, and therefore ensure that their weekends are free from work and either for family time or at least downtime where they are able to go on games consoles if they wish to.

One father once told me of his child who hated school so much that when he got home after a long day of learning, he would shut himself in his bedroom and refuse to come off his games console. His father felt terrible because his son clearly wanted an escape from his difficult days at school, but he knew that the reason his son was finding it so difficult at school was because he wasn't reinforcing his learning from school in his free time after school, therefore he was falling behind and feeling inadequate in comparison to his peers. It was a self-caused vicious cycle. The only time he saw a positive change was when he finally confiscated the games console until his son's grades started to improve.

Though this method may not work for everybody, it should be noted that if you're feeling backed into a corner and like there's no other choice, it's probably because there isn't another choice. If you need to confiscate negatively-impacting technology from your children in order for them to see improvements in their work, then by all means go for it.

It's worth noting however that in a recent survey, almost half of students said that technology for non-educational purposes was distracting [14] so bear that in mind.

105. Managing Your Child's Time Online

Navigating cyberspace can be stressful enough for adults to even comprehend, now imagine what that is like for a child who is vulnerable to all kinds of danger when using the internet. It's essential that you not only support their journey through the treacherous waters of the internet but also navigate alongside them in order to protect and support them as best you can.

Encourage healthy use of digital technology, encourage them to not use technology as a distraction but to use it for its real benefits - education.

The last thing you want is your child to face the real

dangers online, or for them to become addicted to digital distractions, so set them on the right path while learning at home, ensure their homework is as reliable and persuasive as it can possibly be and ensure they feel supported in their educational journeys.

If you feel it necessary, set parental controls and filters on the family computers and digital devices. Observe their conversations on the internet and monitor them in any way you deem appropriate. There's no such thing as being too safe when it comes to looking after your children as they navigate cyberspace.

When it comes to the uncertain world of the internet, there should be no such thing as hands-off parenting, as it will only lead to disaster.

The unique and positive culture of the T.C.E.C centre

At the T.C.E.C centre, we have a qualified teacher take a maximum of 5 students with modern technological facilities to improve learning thereby making it exciting for students to come in after school even on Saturdays.

Ever since the tuition centre began operations, thousands of students in the borough have experienced tremendous educational improvement in their grades as principles have been enacted to help children learn and focus, hence the reason for this book.

The TCEC centre in Hackney has produced excellent GCSE, IGCSE and SATs result every year without fail. At the centre, we teach children between the ages of 6-16 years old reading, English language, English literature, mathematics and spelling. Of course, there are other learning centres that run the same course but it's essential for parents to check the one that suits the child and will bring out the best in him/her. The learning centres use different methods to achieve tremendous results so the method that worked for a child might not work for the other child.

Jack is a smart boy but the learning method he isn't used to is the learning method he is exposed to. As such, he finds it difficult to understand his teachers and he fidget every time. He came to the centre and we introduce him to a step by step program of learning to help him focus on learning activities with rapt attention. His parents were delighted with his progress because he had appeared to be someone who isn't interested in learning activities. He significantly improved at the centre and he moved up 3 grades in just two months. His sister on the other hand prefer the traditional method of learning which made her slow but when she started at the learning centre, she improved and was always eager to do her homework. She is now able to organize herself to carry out her tasks and no longer reluctant to do her homework. Since she used one month to learn addition and two months to learn subtraction, one would think that she would use an additional three months to master timetable but no, Sophia learnt timetable in three weeks. This made division easy for her and when she sat for her SAT test, she had an outstanding result. We worked with her for 80 minutes every week; she had all As' in her GSCE.

A lot of parents expect to see changes in their children within 2-3 weeks of enrolling them in a learning centre. A child who has suffered a considerable learning gap will struggle with learning initially. Parents should understand that children are different and must be treated differently. In the past years, we have developed different lesson plans for children and we have also provided their lesson needs and taught children the best way of learning in order to enhance their learning process.

6

HOW TO DEVELOP AN INQUISITIVE MIND

Once your child enters the education system, they will be exposed to the wonders and the novelty of science. Parents oftentimes neglect this subject at home because it can seem quite intimidating to take on the responsibility of teaching your children the basics behind chemistry, biology and physics. But it certainly does not have to be. Science encourages questions, making observations and forming hypotheses. Part of reducing anxiety and fear of such a subject lies in parents' hands, where your child's preschool years can be spent fostering an inquisitive mind that will be better prepared for tackling scientific subjects in school. This does not necessarily mean enforcing a strict curriculum to cover complicated topics like chemistry, physics, and biology. Instead, there are a number of fun activities to expose your child to and to better prepare them for what's to come. Encouraging inquisitiveness and curiosity stimulates a greater sense of learning within children and developing these skills early-on will benefit your child greatly.

106. Conduct experiments at home

There are a number of experiments that produce exciting results which can be performed using a couple of kitchen items you probably already own combined with the all-important key ingredient of food colouring. These experiments are safe and easy DIYs that will allow you to explain the scientific basis behind reactions and relationships. These new textures, colours and scents are sure to entice your child and encourage new tactile sensations and visual connections. Not only can these experiments produce fun results for your children to explore, the concepts are also straightforward enough for adults to grasp and explain to your children. Recipes along with their scientific explanations can easily be found on the Internet for you to try. A consequence of some of the more elaborate experiments could be a potential mess to clean up afterwards but accept that sometimes exploration can be untidy. Plus, it's a fantastic opportunity to teach your kids responsibility as they clean up after themselves.

Consider the of the following DIY experiments to do with your kids, but don't be afraid to consult the Internet for plenty more ideas to cater to different age ranges:

- Slime: A mixture of glue, saline solution and food colouring will produce a wonderfully squishy and relatively mess-free substance that will entertain your kids for hours.

- Volcano: A tried and tested experiment involving a papier-mâché or playdough volcano encasing a solution of baking soda combined with vinegar that reacts to mimic an eruption.
- Plant growing: Engage in a more long-term observational experiment by growing and cultivating seeds together.
- Magic milk: In a shallow dish, add milk and a few drops of food colouring. Coat the end of a Q-tip with some dish soap and watch a chemical reaction happen as surface tension breaks!
- Baking: Afterall, baking is a science. How do certain ingredients react together to create a cake? Bringing your kids into the kitchen gives them a hands-on experience that yields delicious results.

One mother shared with me that getting her children involved in the kitchen as part of their routine has led to them being more curious about baking in particular. Her sons love baking cakes and decorating them and her strategy has been to get them involved in every step of measuring and mixing while explaining the different ways ingredients work in a cake. It has also been a huge source of bonding between the mother and her sons who would previously spend their afternoons watching TV. This way, they have been able to spend time together and learn something new as the mother continues to nurture her sons' love for baking. For the mother, she said that it required her taking some effort to understand the basic science of baking, but the outcome has been so worth it.

107. TV programs

While we prioritize social interaction in a child's learning, there are also many accessible programs that are both entertaining and educational. The visual aspect captivates children like no other and some of the more dangerous and elaborate experiments that should not be attempted at home are shown in a safe environment. Whether on your favourite streaming service or on an online platform like YouTube which provides free content, TV programs are incredible resources with bright personalities and elaborate explorations that pique your child's interests in the field of science. Make good use of your electronic devices in this way, whether it is your TV or iPad. They are bountiful resources that have ample of benefits when used correctly.

108. Exploring outside

Our surroundings continue to amaze us every day, even well-into adulthood. Get involved with your children by going on walks together and encouraging them to explore their surroundings and discuss the changes they see in the weather, the soil in the ground, the temperature in the air, the insects, etc. Not only are you and your kids escaping outside for fresh air and exercise, but nature is a free source of education that will challenge your children to think and make their own observations. Allow for playful exploration in their surroundings.

As a parent, you don't have to be the adult with an extensive encyclopedia of knowledge. Parents often get nervous and fumble when their children ask questions that they do not know the answer to, which results in the opposite effect by discouraging curiosity and fostering fear in questions. You do not have to immediately gratify them with the correct answer, nor are you expected to. A great way to tackle if you don't know the answer is to ask your child what they might think and bounce ideas between each other and offer to find the answers together. Additionally, know that you, as the parent, are allowed to make mistakes. Treat it as another teachable moment.

109. Encourage discussions

Encourage your children to record their observations, whether in the form of charts, graphs, drawings, or taking photographs. Then ask them to explain their methodologies. This allows your children to develop the ability to communicate and form their own opinions based on observation. It continues to foster an awareness of their surroundings while remaining focused on hands-on tasks. Interacting with world around them and their environment can support their intellectual development, but this needs to be nudged along by parents. Additionally, requiring them to explain their methods allows them the creative freedom, as well as heightens their speaking skills. Children are incredibly perceptive to the emotions of others around them, especially adults. Showing your interest in their work is critical for them to be just as interested in their activities. Encourage your children to make connections, draw parallels, and spot patterns and differences within their own observations.

Some questions you may consider asking:

- What do you think?
- Where else might we see this pattern?
- When does it react this way?
- Why do you think that?
- What would happen if...?

The key here is to listen to the child's answers and respond accordingly.

110. Invest in a few inexpensive pieces of equipment

Without having to break the bank, you can certainly improve all of the aforementioned activities by purchasing some inexpensive tools catered for children's use that will do wonders for their imagination and engagement. Consider investing in an inexpensive microscope that will take observational activities to another level. Implement the strategies of encouraging discussions and recordings to further enhance the learning experience. If DIY isn't your thing, bookstores, toy stores, and variety shops often stock simple age-appropriate science kits within a range of topics to get your kids busy learning for a few hours. These kits maintain a hands-on learning approach and builds upon skills they already have in perhaps a more advanced way. They also give children enough agency to safely conduct experiments with minimal adult intervention, which motivates them and keeps them engaged.

111. Make use of science centers and museums

Kids usually get discounts at centers and museums that, more often than not, have specific programs catered to their age group. It's a great way to have an exciting day out and experience exhibits and fascinating technology in person. Science centers have a wide range of new topics to discover; from the galaxy, to the human body, to the real creatures that may roam in rainforests today, to creatures of the past that are now extinct. The boundaries are endless. Science centers are a great place to foster wonder and curiosity. While these outings won't realistically be regular occurrences, they are an amazing reward for your kids within their learning journey that also won't break the bank. It is also equally a great place for adults to enjoy themselves and maybe even learn a thing or two!

7

CREATIVE OUTLETS FOR KIDS

Fostering creativity in children is often easier than parents may think. Parents have a full plate and are responsible for a slew of things within their children's development that often unintentionally take precedence over creative thinking. However, fostering creative thinking from an early age will end up serving them beyond their childhood years because of its ability to allow kids to think more abstractly and fluidly. This will follow them well-into adulthood where successful critical thinking and problem-solving is often contingent on thinking outside of the box. Nurturing your child's creativity comes in a myriad of forms. There are plenty of activities to do in order to encourage free thinking and foster imagination. Many of these activities rely on parents taking a hands-off approach, rather than the opposite. But when children are allowed to think freely without constant surveillance is when the best art is created.

112. Designate a creative space

This by no means has to be an elaborate playroom. Parents often think that the creative arts will break the bank but sometimes keeping it simple has the exact effect you may be after. Designating a space (whether it's a small corner or spot on the dining table) where children can be imaginative and think beyond their spaces gives them the power to think freely. Consider placing some tools like paper, crayons, and modelling clay. Children oftentimes require encouragement and positive reinforcement, so join them in their activities and tap into your own imagination by telling stories and drawing pictures to show them that there are no boundaries and playing pretend is a good thing. Modelling your own creative outlets in front of your children encourages them to embrace these activities as well. If your children are older, offer them a prompt and tell them to interpret it however they like. The activities can be as simplistic as you desire and do not require a lot of preplanning and preparation.

Particularly for children who get distracted easily and have a hard time concentrating on their studies, carving out a space for them where their activities and curriculum are not as rigid gives them the independence and freedom to let loose and not be as confined within structure, while still being productive and continuously thinking. It gives students who are not as keen on studying a time to look forward to. This is also the exact time to avoid overparenting and micromanaging your kids as it's critical to facilitate their creativity without stifling them.

113. Allow kids to be bored

It may sound counterintuitive, but with so many activities to keep your kids constantly busy and preoccupied, giving them a chance to get bored allows them to think of their own ways to entertain themselves. A lack of simulation and distraction makes children more motivated to think outside of the box and come up with their own ways to occupy their time. Remember that children too can experience burnout from overscheduling and the onslaught of too many activities. This downtime is just as important as school, extracurriculars, chores, and time spent on electronic devices. Scheduling downtime in between all of the hecticness that is usually a child's life enables the parent to prioritize it between everything else that is going on and remember to do so on a daily basis. Imagination and creativity blossom from a child's boredom as they come up with new and exciting activities on their own, rather than parents and teachers constantly supplying entertainment and simulation.

114. Put on a play or performance

Tell your children to come up with a story to put a play or performance on, whether it is with their siblings or with their toys. Giving them an open-ended activity like a performance will allow them to take risks. Getting your children into storytelling is a fantastic way for them to channel their imagination in a loosely structured way, while the performance aspect gives them a chance to share and celebrate their ideas before an audience. This instills a sense of taking leadership and ownership over their creations and its execution and is an opportunity to practice their communication skills and public speaking, even before their immediate family. For children who are often inattentive, this gives them a chance to channel their focus into something independently and have autonomy in their projects. While every child is different, seeing and understanding where your children thrive in is a great way to channel their focus.

One father shared with me that he noticed his son had an affinity for music and son. And so, being perceptive to what his son thrived in, the father began giving his son opportunities to perform his own dances in front of his family. This has opened up a newfound confidence within him that has led to his son pursuing theatre in his free time. His skills have branched off into singing as well as improving his dancing, in order to perform in bigger productions in front of real audiences. The parent shared that this brought out his personality even more before his family as well as in school, where he isn't as afraid of new social interactions and public speaking.

115. Read with your children

Reading with your children is a tried and true method to cultivate your children's natural capacity to use their imaginations. It's a great way to bond with your children one on one. Parents love acting out scenes from books with funny voices to engage their children into the stories. Some parents read along with their children to further their comprehension as they reach the age. Not only does carving out time to read out loud with your child everyday give them something else to look forward to, but it is also a great way to increase discipline and concentration. Very rarely are children engaged for long periods of time but committing to regular reading times may introduce a new habit of quiet and thoughtful time. It may take some time for your kids to get used to, but parents can agree that reading time is enjoyable for both the child and the parent as it also fosters a special bond. Reading from an early age also nurtures a lifelong love for stories and learning and thus expanding your child's horizons. There are plenty of books within each age range, so you are bound to find something to suit your child's interests and needs. Additionally, there are a number of books that tackle heavy subjects like racism and bullying that are available for you to use to educate your children in a simple and succinct way. Many parents are often nervous to tackle the serious subject matter but rely on these picture books to handle the topics sensitively and appropriately for their children to understand.

116. Beneficial screen time

With technology on the rise, parents find it increasingly difficult to avoid screen time when it comes to occupying their children. Whether it is time spent on the computer or a tablet, the Internet is an amazing resource to get your children thinking creatively with music, dance, and arts. The challenge really lies in finding apps and programs that are committed to educating your children, as well as stimulating their imagination. Monitoring their screen time and making sure the content they are consuming is crucial. A simple search online will expose you to a myriad of apps that are teacher-approved and feature carefully curated videos and activities that explore interesting topics to engage your kids in drawing, dancing, and crafts. Additionally, there are plenty of drawing apps that provide a blank slate for your children to explore digital art on.

Parents have found that doing arts and crafts with their kids are a fun way for the adult and child to get involved together. The challenge for parents is striking a balance of media consumption and time spent away from screens.

Ways to ensure quality screen time:

- Develop your own rules for screen time that will best suit your child. Some kids do well with one hour of screen time, while others benefit from more broken up in intervals throughout the day.
- Create tech-free times like during dinner time, especially for older children.
- Seek out interactive content that gets your children thinking, rather than just passively watching.
- Make use of parental controls and preview programs and apps to ensure they feature appropriate content.
- Be wary of advertisements and educate your children on what they are.
- Encourage your children to think critically about what they see on their screens and discuss what they have learned.
- As your children get older, educate them on the appropriate behaviours expected of them on when engaging on the Internet, like cyberbullying and sharing personal information.
- Set an example to your children and limit your own screen time as well.

117. Learning a new language

Children soak new information up like a sponge. At a younger age, the preadolescent brain is able to grasp new languages far more quickly than adults. Not only will a new language stimulate their mind, but simply exposing them to new sounds and inflections exposes them to a broader environment and will be immensely helpful in their future, should they decide to seriously pursue more languages. More importantly, learning a new language gives children another way to express themselves and nurtures creativity, flexibility and better engagement in problem solving. Creativity does not only lie in arts and crafts, but also lies in language learning as well as it fosters the very habits that encourage creativity in more traditional areas. It stimulates the brain and encourages children to use their memories. Being exposed to language and subsequently a new culture at a young age fosters a different perspective for your child.

Parents have found that by simply watching language learning programs on TV, they have witnessed their children being far more open and accepting to new sights and sounds, especially in multilingual environments. They have noticed that their children are far more engaged in their surroundings and in social interactions, despite not understanding the new language completely. It has done wonders for broadening their horizons as they have a better cross-cultural understanding and are therefore far more empathetic.

A mother very recently told me that enrolling her daughter in Japanese classes along with watching Japanese cartoons online has encouraged the whole family to speak in their mother-tongue. While everyone is quite rusty, the mother shared that encouraging her daughter to pursue the language ended up having the bigger effect of bringing them all closer to their Japanese heritage, which was an unexpected bonus for the whole family. Now, the daughter practices speaking Japanese with her family while attending classes and has been advancing at a rapid rate because she is so enthusiastic and motivated to learn the language. The mother also takes her daughter to their Japanese supermarket to expose her to another environment where she can identify her second language. For the mother, seeing her child's confidence grow as she is able to express herself in multiple languages has been exciting to see.

118. Make use of music

Children love music and it's a great tool to benefit their creative development. For children, music is much more than simply just listening to it. They enjoy interacting with music by singing, clapping, and dancing. Instead of listening to the same nursery rhymes over and over again, expose your kids to the variety of sounds that exist. Purchasing or even making your own DIY instruments to play along with is great way to help train your child's musical ear. Choose a variety of songs that have a range of rhythms and contrast between each other to show new, exciting styles that will help them learn the diversity that exists better. Include your own favourite tunes and expose your children to the joy of music. You can take this a step further by encouraging your children to come up with their own music. Composing and developing their own lyrics is a sure way to get their creative juices flowing. Foster their creative urges and push them to pursue their creative whims.

119. Get active with dance

Music and dance go hand in hand. Children naturally want to move and expel their energy. A great way to structure their mobility and focus on performance is by dancing. Parents can choose to enroll their students in official dance lessons or take a more laid-back approach by spending some time during the day simply moving to music. Having a structured approach by pursuing dance taught by a professional has a great many benefits. Similarly, taking a break in the middle of the day to simply let loose and move your bodies can boost productivity and focus afterwards. Dance has a number of benefits that will creatively stimulate your child as it uses the body to communicate ideas. It involves coordination, endurance, and a greater range of motion, compared to other creatively charged activities. If you decide to approach dance in a more relaxed way and simply dancing to music is not enough, there is a library of choreography online made specifically for children that will challenge and show them how to express themselves with bodily movement.

120. Offer reinforcement that is conducive to their learning

As much as you want your kids to know that their artwork is the best, you might want to consider instead asking them to explain their work and encouraging them to talk about their artwork. Children respond to positive reinforcement and the idea here is not to discourage them, but to teach them to speak confidently about their work. Ask specific questions and avoid giving generic compliments to get them hooked on receiving praise for everything they do. Fear of failure stems from this and can lead to stifling creativity and motivation to pursue the unknown. Instead, encourage conversation about their artwork and explore their process and perhaps acknowledge how hard they may have worked on the piece.

What you might say to a child about their artwork:

- I see you coloured this pink. Why did you choose that colour?
- Tell me about this drawing you made.
- Did you have fun making it?
- I like the lines/dots/squiggles that you made here.

PLEASE LEAVE A 1-CLICK REVIEW!

Thank you for reading this book and engaging in the next step to establish healthy and effective child learning. I hope these tips help you in the same way they have helped many others.

I would really appreciate if you could take 60 seconds to write a short review for this book on Amazon, even if it's just a few sentences! Your help in spreading the word is greatly appreciated. Reviews from readers like you make a huge difference in helping new readers find helpful books like this one. I joyfully read every single review.

Just click on the link below and you will be taken straight to the review page on Amazon.

Thank you!

Bukky Ekine Ogunlana

101 Tips
for
Helping With Your Child's Learning

Proven Strategies for Accelerated Learning and Raising
Smart Children Using Positive Parenting Skills

BUKKY EKINE-OGUNLANA

Review Book Here

CONCLUSION

Thank you for buying the book - 101 Tips for Helping with Your child's learning. I hope this book has taught you different strategies, methods and ways to help your child's learning. Parenting is a noble calling and raising children who are successful both at home and school is not an easy task. I hope this book will make your duty as a parent to make your child successful at school less daunting. I hope that this book will make your dream of raising a brilliant and well-behaved student come true.

Remember, the best students at school are not the ones who simply study before an exam or can just write a good essay, the best students are the ones who are willing to put the work in daily in order to succeed. Your children cannot achieve this alone though, and that is the message you should take away from this book. Your role in their learning is just as important as their role.

Help guide their educational journeys and reinforce the lessons they are being taught at school and you're well on your way to effectively assisting with your child's journey to learning and success.

Whether you're training your child for a life as a scientist, writer, doctor or even actor, understand what skills they need and help keep them on track.

Before you go off and help your children with their educational journeys, please do leave us some feedback for the book. Whether it's a review out of five or genuine, constructive feedback on what you liked, disliked or would have taken a different approach with. Let us know!

Now, here's to your children turning out to be future leaders and pioneers in their respective fields!

Cheers!!!

OTHER BOOKS YOU'LL LOVE!

CLICK ON THE BOOKS

Link to Book

96 | OTHER BOOKS YOU'LL LOVE!

Link to Book

Link to Book

OTHER BOOKS YOU'LL LOVE! | 97

[Link to Book](#)

[Link to Book](#)

98 | OTHER BOOKS YOU'LL LOVE!

Link to Book

Link to Book

OTHER BOOKS YOU'LL LOVE! | 99

Link to Book

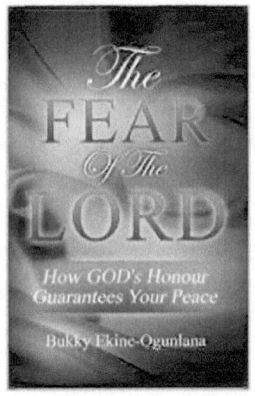

Link to Book

100 | OTHER BOOKS YOU'LL LOVE!

Link to Book

Link to Book

OTHER BOOKS YOU'LL LOVE! | 101

Link to Book

OTHER BOOKS YOU'LL LOVE!

[Link to Book](#)

YOUR FREE GIFT!

As a way of saying thank your for
purchasing this book, I am
offer offering you a free
parenting book!

You can click on the link
below or you can wait until
the end of the book to collect
and download your free
copy.

[DOWNLOAD YOUR FREE COPY HERE](#)

REFERENCES

1. http://www.pownallgreen.stockport.sch.uk/wp-content/uploads/2014/07/Helping-your-child-learn.pdf
2. https://www.linkedin.com/pulse/benefits-helping-children-homework-elliott-shostak
3. https://www2.ed.gov/parents/academic/help/homework/
4. https://www.babycentre.co.uk/a6509/developmental-milestones-hearing
5. https://freekidsbooks.org/wp-content/uploads/2016/12/Teaching-Children-to-Read.pdf
6. http://www.parentingcounts.org/information/documents/talking-to-baby-100-705-200907.pdf
7. http://ftp.iza.org/dp7416.pdf
8. https://ryanlanz.com/2015/05/06/why-you-should-encourage-your-children-to-tell-stories/

9. https://ahrc.eq.edu.au/ourservices/Documents/rc-parent-booklet.pdf
10. https://centerforparentingeducation.org/library-of-articles/focus-parents/role-model-promise-peril/
11. https://mrswintersbliss.com/fiction-vs-nonfiction-teaching-ideas/
12. https://pdfs.semanticscholar.org/aed9/5c4d2b4ddb11d4199e4ab91ac0ee41fb2219.pdf
13. https://www.cameverlands.org.uk/10-benefits-of-reading/
14. https://www.insidehighered.com/digital-learning/article/2019/07/10/survey-shows-nearly-half-students-distracted-technology

USEFUL WEBSITES:

1. http://taylorda01.weebly.com/increasingly-difficult-questions.html - really good for increasingly difficult questions
2. www.mathsbot.com – brilliant GCSE styles questions http://www.mrbartonmaths.com/teachers/ - endless amounts of resources
3. https://justmaths.co.uk/2015/12/21/9-1-exam-questions-by-topic-higher-tier/ - exam style questions for higher tier (worked solutions as well)
4. https://justmaths.co.uk/2015/11/29/9-1-exam-

questions-by-topic-foundation-version-2/ - exactly the same as above but for foundation
5. https://www.missbsresources.com/ - some useful revision mats
6. https://www.resourceaholic.com/ - lots of resources and thought provoking activities
7. http://bland.in/edexcel_9-1.html - exam questions
8. https://www.mathsgenie.co.uk/ - past papers
9. https://corbettmaths.com/contents/ - exam style questions
10. https://www.maths4everyone.com/ - lots of loop cards, exam questions
11. https://www.accessmaths.co.uk/ - some great starters on here and lots of other resources
12. https://www.teachitmaths.co.uk/ - lots of different activities
13. https://www.cimt.org.uk/projects/mep/index.htm - challenging worded problems
14. https://www.math-salamanders.com/ - some useful worksheets (have to have a hunt)
15. https://nrich.maths.org/ - brilliant problem solving resources and thought provoking activities

www.ingramcontent.com/pod-product-compliance
Lightning Source LLC
Chambersburg PA
CBHW021156080526
44588CB00008B/362